THE *official* ROYAL BEDSIDE BOOK

Javelin Books

POOLE · NEW YORK · SYDNEY

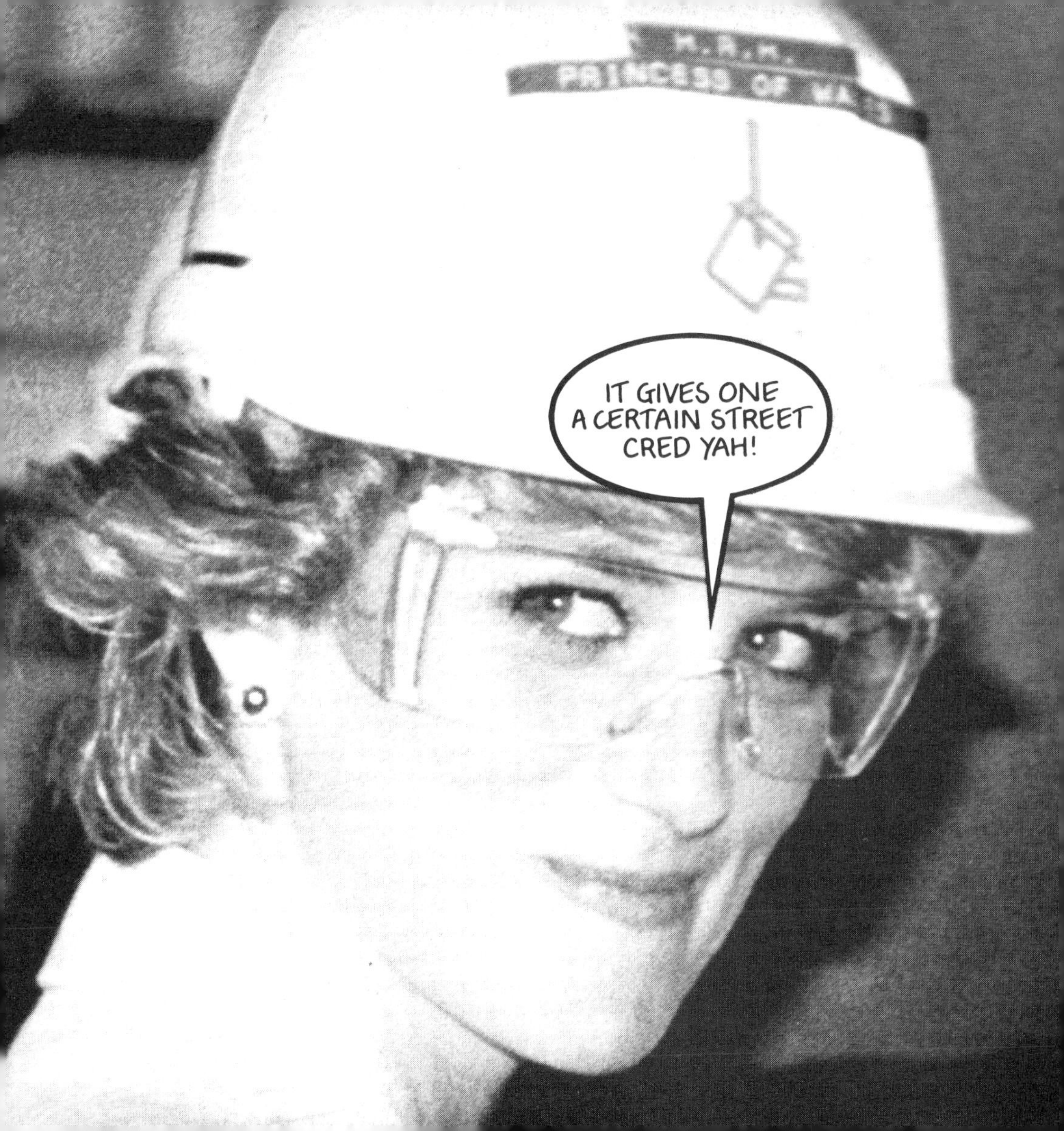
H.R.H.
PRINCESS OF
IT GIVES ONE
A CERTAIN STREET
CRED YAH!

I'M TELLING YOU... HER PROGRAMME'S STUCK
THEN PUSH THE MANUAL OVERRIDE

First published in the UK 1986 by Javelin Books,
Link House, West Street, Poole, Dorset, BH15 1LL

Copyright © 1986 Blandford Press
Photographs: Popperfoto
Designed: Mark Smith
Picture selection & captions: J G (& colleagues)

Distributed in Australia by
Capricorn Link (Australia) Pty Ltd,
PO Box 665, Lane Cove, NSW 2066

British Library Cataloguing in Publication Data

The Royal Bedside book.
  828'.91409   PN6231.R6

ISBN 0-7137-1877-3

The publisher accepts no responsibility for the 20th century to date, the Common Market
wine lake, Ronald Reagan (again) or anyone's lost knighthood or MBE.

Coming soon: Yet Another Royal Baby Book

Printed in Great Britain by
R. J. Acford Ltd., Chichester, Sussex.